Pushing Back the Ocean

Tide Turning Leadership Lessons

By

KARL BIMSHAS

BIMMEDIA

San Diego, California

PUBLISHED BY

BIMMEDIA

San Diego, California

ISBN 978-1-4116-9703-4

*Photo Credits: Photographs of Nauset Beach from the
private collections of John Bimshas; Dave Mills;
Lee Quincy and Jan Schneider*

Contents

Contents

Dedication

For Karen,

and to all of those who have had the courage to

push back the ocean of naysayers and doubters

during their journey from goal to goal.

Introduction

Tide Turning

It's amazing to me the number of people I have come across who do not appear to put any thought or action into their lives. They float about, rudderless, just drifting with the tide and changing winds. They react, occasionally, to events thrust before them – but they seldom, if ever, act on purpose.

Then there is the ambitious but discontented lot. The people who know they can get more out of life, but don't know how to begin. They may have walked along the wet sand and dampened their bare feet to test the waters, but they have not yet committed to the personal changes they need to make. Those not accustomed to planning their success can find the odds overwhelming. They are in constant danger of being swamped by the unrelenting negative waves of "don't", followed by "can't", followed by "shouldn't". Is it any wonder that so few practice and learn the skills required for standing upright and persevering?

It is my contention that more people must find the strength and discipline to focus on improvement, wherever improvements can be made. We do not need to accept mediocrity and poor leadership, either in ourselves or in others. We can begin to treasure the gifts we have been given. The lessons contained in these pages offer a way. If applied regularly, you will notice that step-by-step, you are able to turn the tide.

Lesson One

Goals

Not much in your life gets achieved without beginning as a goal. Yes, happenstance can play a role and serendipity adds flavor. But it is the goal, the steadfast, thought through determination that leads to accomplishment. Well-spent hours build into days, into months, into years, into a lifetime filled with high achievement.

We are blessed because we intuitively know when we've discovered a compelling goal. Our pulse quickens and adrenaline pulls us toward it with an astonishing force.

Once, on a late December morning, I decided to stroll along Nauset Beach, one of the most breathtaking stretches of sand to be found on Cape Cod. The late year wind was cold but refreshing.

Not much in your life gets achieved without beginning as a goal.

The mark we leave on the earth is indeed temporary, but it may be longer lasting than we think.

As I strolled along the shoreline I occasionally glanced over my shoulder to spy my solitary footprints in the sand. I was walking without purpose at first, just trying to clear the fog in my head. At the time I was uncomfortably conscious of the fact that I wasn't sure if the tide was coming in or going out.

I had noticed an object away in the distance, and I recall closing my coat tighter around my neck and thinking to myself, "Well, I'm not going to walk *that* far. It's too cold." After a short while I began to think about the footprints behind me and imagined the waves washing them away. That made me consider further, like many have before when leaving footprints, how temporary our time is, and how we should relish each step in our journey. Soon that object in the distance appeared much closer and I enthusiastically thought, "Yeah, let's go for it."

I picked up my pace, and then almost immediately found myself sprinting. I heard the hard sand crunching beneath my shoes and felt the biting coastal New England wind cutting across my face. To my dismay, the object turned out to be a large piece of unexciting driftwood. As I disappointedly circled the lackluster discovery, I was also relieved to confirm it was not the carcass of a hapless marine animal. When I turned around I abruptly confronted my earlier solitary set of footprints, still intact.

Looking down the long stretch of beach I could tell that at first they meandered, gently brushing the surface, then they straightened and dug deeper into the sand at the point I decided to investigate the washed up wood. It was then I realized that the tide was indeed going out and my steps would be preserved a few hours more.

I decided to follow them as a path to return to my car in the parking lot. It didn't take long before I noticed that I wasn't matching my footprints step for step. At first I weaved back and forth over my original route, but ultimately my new steps were coursing closer to the water's edge. Yes, the tide was receding, but the tracks I left made it appear as if I were pushing back the ocean. This was a very interesting experience for me, analogous to the pursuit of goals and life itself.

The mark we leave on the earth is indeed temporary, but it may be longer lasting than we think. You may choose to meander through the day without purpose if you'd like, but when you pick a goal that you can see, you can't help but race for it. Once you reach your destination, make the time to reflect, to see how far you've come. Although you may want to retrace your steps, you won't be able to match them exactly because the conditions have changed as new goals present themselves. And you will find yourself, if only fleetingly, pushing back the ocean. What a beautiful experience and with contemplation, a wonderfully empowering gift from God!

Nothing happens

unless first a dream.

– Carl Sandburg

Lesson Two

Vision Passion Action

I once worked for a fortune 500 company that had a division committed to continuous learning. That was an oddity for a conservative white-shirted firm, but in time this experimental learning organization grew into a two billion dollar juggernaut. Sadly, as often happens in large corporations when fresh success is pitted against the status quo, this outstanding organization began to be picked apart by an unenlightened and apprehensive headquarters through mergers, consolidations and a type of management gentrifying. It was before the administrative pruning that I was first exposed to two-time Olympic Pentathlete, Marilyn

King's "Olympian Thinking", a formula I adopted immediately and have attempted to live up to ever since. If only the company that sponsored her talk had done the same, it may have been able to avoid losing half a decade caught in a panic mode of fighting to survive, and instead been in a growth mode and learning how to thrive.

Nothing great in the world has been accomplished without passion.

- Georg Wilhelm

A vision without

action is called

a daydream; but then

again, action without

a vision

is called a nightmare.

- Jim Sorensen

Exceptional Performance

If you search the world for the regular, the uninspired and the tiresome you will find yourself joining many others in a r.u.t. Most can only see what they look for. If you can modify your thinking, you can realize much more. To achieve *exceptional performance* you need the magical combination of vision, passion and action.

Vision + Passion + Action

= Exceptional Performance

Vision is what you imagine and think about. What you see in your mind. Worriers see failure. High achievers only see success.

Passion is what stirs you forward. Those who routinely accomplish goals have a burning desire to complete their mission. It is what gets them up in the morning and keeps them up late into the night.

Action is the execution of your plan. It is the actual day-to-day work that nourishes the vision and passion.

Those who regularly demonstrate all three elements of vision, passion and action, are the ones who accomplish superior results.

We see the elements of this formula everyday, but often it is incomplete.

It is the *daydreamer* who has passion and vision, but lacks action.

The *workaholic* has tremendous action and passion, but without vision they eventually find themselves accomplishing things that are of no value to them.

Those with vision and action but no passion accomplish *mediocrity*.

Unfortunately, it's this last group that probably best describes most of the people you encounter.

*To achieve **exceptional** **performance** you need the magical combination of vision, passion and action.*

I believe that those who can arouse and maintain the passion in others while sustaining it in themselves are distinguished as authentic leaders. The world has far too few of these people, yet your help can begin to make a big difference.

Get action.

Seize the moment.

Man was never

intended to be an

oyster.

-Theodore Roosevelt

You can begin making a positive difference by first helping others rediscover their passion.

Lesson Three

Helping others discover their passion

I found that after achieving a few of my own early goals, success began to become a habit. There were times when I felt so jazzed that nothing could've held me back. On the downside, I was slowly growing impatient with the people around me. It seemed to me that no one was moving fast enough. I was frustrated because as far as I was concerned, other people were not accomplishing much and it started to really tick me off. What I needed to realize was that other people were not making the same self-discoveries that I was. I soon learned I had to change my approach toward the people I interacted with. It wasn't complicated and only required the investment of well-spent time. For me, helping those who want to work on their own personal development feeds my soul. One of the greatest ways you can begin making a positive difference is by first helping others rediscover their passion.

Using The Power Question

Start by asking one question that combines a servant leadership mentality with a focus on results. I call it, *"The Power Question"* because it carries a lot of clout. It contains the results driven muscle of helpfulness, compassion, and empowerment in learning what is truly important to others.

Here it is:

"What one thing can I do for you that will most help you make a positive difference?"

If you come across someone who is unfocused, ineffective or troubled, lost in a tizzy of disorder or stalled with confusion, ask him or her *The Power Question.* It requires them to slow down and assess how you and your abilities could best help them. You are forcing them to delegate a task to you that must be positive in nature, or at the very least lead to a positive outcome.

Once determined, honor their request -- after all you asked for it. Accomplishing that mission will, at a minimum make you feel like a million bucks because you acted unselfishly and will no doubt have been of great service to the recipient.

With some people you may need help getting them started. Begin brainstorming together and eventually you'll both be able to come across a very good idea that will help the other person positively move forward. Those deep in disarray could give you an ill-conceived knee-jerk response. Just coax them gently with the clarification, "Will that *best* help you make a *positive* difference?" They will ultimately respond with what they think you can do for them and they'll appreciate the attention you're giving them.

If you ever find yourself stuck and unsure of what to do next, go to someone, anyone and ask *The Power Question*. You will always get an answer and the request may surprise you. Acting on that request will serve to help move at least two people forward towards their goal.

People of a certain age undoubtedly remember the yearly joy of watching, the Rankin Bass television special, "Santa Claus is Comin' to Town". It's the animated story of how Kris Kringle got his start, narrated by Fred Astaire with Mickey Rooney providing the voice of Santa Claus.

Who can forget the frightening Winter Warlock whose icy demeanor is melted by a choo choo train and the kindness of young Kris Kringle?

Winter, unsure his changed outlook on life will last, is encouraged by Kris, the woodland creatures and an infectious song, that declares making a change is as easy as putting "one foot in front of the other."

There is great truth in that simplicity. People often make many excuses as to why change is not possible. They fret over their personal concerns. They spend energy worrying about how they will conduct all the changes being asked of them. Eventually they grow anxious, wondering what type of impact their efforts will have. The only thing all of this angst creates is inactivity. At the end of the day, all it takes it a little movement in approximately the right direction.

Put one foot in front of the other
And soon you'll be walking cross the floor
Put one foot in front of the other
And soon you'll be walking out the door

You never will get where you're going
If you never get up on your feet
Come on, there's a good tail wind blowing
A fast walking man is hard to beat

If you want to change your direction
If your time of life is at hand
Well don't be the rule be the exception
A good way to start is to stand

--Jules Bass

Quite often the very

act of helping another

has the pleasant side

effect of resolving your

own troubles

simultaneously.

I'm not advocating that you break out into a song and dance routine everytime you offer to help someone (though if that works for you, go for it), but being able to help someone when you are having difficulties is one of the best medicines available. Quite often the very act of helping another has the pleasant side effect of resolving your own troubles simultaneously. You frequently find your problem to be insignificant when matched against that of another. In some instances, time spent away from your own problem gives your mind a chance to work on it -- without your well meaning but solution sapping interruptions.

Sometimes the lessons you learn while helping someone else can be applied to your own problem. Sincerely posing *The Power Question* will create both a positive and proactive feeling in yourself, the likes of which you may have never experienced before.

Try to get in the habit of asking T*he Power Question* of someone different everyday. You'll be enhancing relationships and in no time building a reputation as a helpful problem solver.

Using Reflective Questions

Now, keep that momentum by asking a series of reflective questions that can provide a needed boost of passion that will ignite those you are helping and carry them forward.

The first question to ask;

"Why are you still here, doing what you're doing?"

Keep probing until one or more of these three intrinsic motivators is revealed.

For ***personal development,***
which sounds like, "I learn so much here."

Because of ***enriching experiences*** with others,
which sounds like, "I love the people here."

Or to work on ***leaving a legacy,***
which sounds like, "I want to help make things better here."

When people can understand what motivates them, they can do more of it. If someone is able to identify with one of these motivations, they only need to recognize it and continue working on it in order to rekindle some passion.

Using Learning Styles

The next activity to help be most effective is to identify which learning style is preferred. People learn new things in different ways. Knowing which way they like best can make accomplishing new tasks easier.

Determining a primary learning style.

Is it **Action-Oriented?** Are you likely to roll up your sleeves and get to it, preferring to learn through trial and error?

Are you **People-Oriented?** Do you like to confer with others who may have experienced the problem prior to you?

Or are you **Information-Oriented?** Are you among the first to look for the training manual or some type of documentation you can refer to frequently?

To be most effective,

it's helpful to find out

which learning style is

preferred.

I'm a combination of an Information and Action Learner. When confronting a new task I tend to skim any documentation then roll up my sleeves and start tinkering. If I get really stumped I'll call on others for advice. Some people can choose one style very easily, while others have trouble picking from the three. If it's hard to determine between two choices, either will probably be successful. This person has the flexibility of learning equally well regardless of the environment. However, most do have a preference. For example, giving an Action Learner a 200-page technical document to read, or parachuting an Information Learner into a room full of strangers will not likely lead to success.

Using The Three Legged Stool

It's important to recognize that when leading, be it a household, classroom, civic group, rock band or corporation, it's vital to strike a balance and be equally successful in three areas:

Customer Satisfaction,

> *how satisfied are the people you serve?*

Employee Satisfaction,

> *how do you treat those who help you serve?*

Profitable Revenue Growth.

> *Money, and the ability to make, save and reinvest it is a crucial part of any organization.*

These are the three legs to the stool of a successful enterprise. You rest your entire enterprise on this stool each day. Eventually, either wear and tear or neglect begins to show. The moment you notice the stool beginning to wobble - fix the irregular leg. If you don't, the condition will worsen and you run the risk of one day unexpectedly being pitched off the stool or worse, collapsing it completely. Now ask;

"In which of these areas do you feel you could make the greatest positive impact?"

The people who work on the things they most want to work on tend to get the most done.

Using An Action Question

Review all the previous questions and answers up to this point and close in on the final question;

"What are you going to do tomorrow to get started?"

Find common themes that can act as a thread, weaving several goals together and hold yourself and others to the commitments made. Be open to the answers and make it your mission to fulfill the requests of anyone who is brave enough to provide you with honest feedback.

Never doubt that a small group of thoughtful, committed citizens can change the world. Indeed, it is the only thing that ever has.

-Margaret Mead

Few will have the greatness to bend history; but each of us can work to change a small portion of events ... It is from numberless diverse acts of courage and belief that human history is thus shaped. Each time a man stands up for an ideal, or acts to improve the lot of others, or strikes out against injustice, he sends forth a tiny ripple of hope.

- Robert F. Kennedy

Lesson Four

Change a piece of the world

It doesn't take as much to change the world as many may think. Anytime you interact with others, it's impossible not to have a type of influence on them in some way. The first thing to do is define your world, or more specifically, your slice of the world. We are each given a figurative plot of earth to work with. Some are blessed with fertile ground while others are laden with rock and clay. We don't always find them right away, but all of us are also equipped with the perfect set of tools for the job at hand. It is how we marry those tools with the plot we are given that will determine what each of us is able to harvest. Some hoard and some help. Some squander while others appear to make miracles happen. Those who "get it" soon realize that it is better to be flexible and adapt to changing conditions. The farmer who throws a birthday party for his daughter in the middle of a drought is going to be able to turn the sudden bursting storm cloud of rain into a positive event. In the end it is about responsibility and how you choose to cultivate your own garden.

It doesn't take as much to change the world as many may think.

Life's Purpose

You are not here merely to make a living. You are here in order to enable the world to live more amply, with greater vision, with a finer spirit of hope and achievement. You are here to enrich the world, and you impoverish yourself if you forget the errand.

- *Woodrow Wilson*

Men make history, and not the other way around. In periods where there is no leadership, society stands still. Progress occurs when courageous, skillful leaders seize the opportunity to change things for the better.

-Harry S Truman

If you are going to be an effective "farmer" then you will probably encounter change and you will need to help others change too. Not an easy task because most people dislike change. It can be very uncomfortable. I personally have found that I tend to resist change unless I am involved in creating it. That revelation allowed me to stumble into one of the great secrets of change. Get yourself involved and help others get involved. Always be prepared to lead change. The ride is usually more fun from the front seat.

Lead forward and help create enduring change

Be forthright and simply tell people what to expect. Knowing what the change is helps people prepare for it. Those who create elaborate tales or engage in deceitful spin ultimately experience triple strikes. They hurt the people involved, they discredit themselves and they sabotage the change itself. Embrace what's positive and present the facts. Deliver anything less than that and you risk being swept under by a current of concern and confusion.

Encourage all those affected to get together to foster a sense of camaraderie. When someone knows they are not the only one feeling uneasy there is quicker bonding with their cohorts. This leads to greater joint involvement in trying to cope with the shift to their routine.

Think of how quickly college freshmen are able to form friendships that may last a lifetime. They share a variety of experiences that bond them together. Once together, people may commiserate, and some may struggle or become melancholy. It's okay; let them have a little time to mentally give up whatever it is they need to in order to make room for the change.

People have a tendency to self limit and focus on what can't be done. Don't let them fall into that snare. Cut through the net of negative beliefs. They may be tangled in a jumble of competing priorities. Eventually they will sort through them and discover what's truly important.

Once the priorities are clarified, people will begin to doubt they have enough resources available to participate in the change. Your job is to help them find those resources, be they internal or external. Recognize that people change at different speeds, but they do change. Keep at it. Keep the focus on the goal, make sure an old habit has been replaced with a new one and monitor the results. If you let up too soon people will lapse into their old ways.

Take care of your own house. Doing so exceptionally well will in no small part change the world in ways you may never fully appreciate. Apply the leadership lessons often and you will soon learn that you have the ability to push back the ocean.

Summary

B elow you will find a summary of the tide turning leadership lessons that can help you and the people you care about change your outlook on any given situation.

- Find purpose. Race for your goals and reflect once you achieve them.
- Be exceptional. Live with vision, passion and action.
- Help others discover their passions and help them make a positive difference.
- Uncover the motivating factors that keep you doing what you are doing.
- Make learning easier by using the style that is most comfortable for you.

- Take action on the areas where you can make the greatest contribution.

- Change a piece of the world.

About the Author

Karl Bimshas is driven to lead and inspire others to maximize their unique strengths and continuously improve themselves, their organization and society, by bringing the powers of vision, passion and action to each endeavor. He believes doing so will help positively energize our nation and contribute to greater peace, prosperity, fun, understanding, responsibility and liberty in the world.

With a M.S. in Executive Leadership from the University of San Diego and a B.A. in Mass Communication from Emerson College in Boston, Karl Bimshas has held several operational and sales leadership positions in public and private corporations. He currently lives in Southern California with his wife and two children. Learn more at www.KarlBimshas.com

Give the Gift.
Help Turn the Tide!
Additional copies of Pushing Back the Ocean: Tide Turning Leadership Lessons are available via Lulu.com, Amazon.com, and other booksellers for $9.95 each

www.ingramcontent.com/pod-product-compliance
Lightning Source LLC
Chambersburg PA
CBHW021920170526
45157CB00005B/2119